DO IT YOURSELF PLAYGROUNDS

BY M. PAUL FRIEDBERG

THE ARCHITECTURAL PRESS LTD
LONDON

ISBN (CLOTH EDITION) 0 85139 174 5

(PAPER EDITION) 0 85139 174 3

© 1975 M. PAUL FRIEDBERG

FIRST PUBLISHED IN GREAT BRITAIN IN 1976 BY
THE ARCHITECTURAL PRESS LTD.

PRINTED IN GREAT BRITAIN BY
R.J. ACFORD LTD., CHICHESTER, SUSSEX

ACKNOWLEDGEMENTS

SPECIAL THANKS TO VINCENT TROCCHIA WITHOUT WHOSE ASSISTANCE
THIS BOOK WOULD NOT HAVE BEEN POSSIBLE.

ALSO TO TOM MOHR, BONNIE ROCHE, CYNTHIA RICE AND MY SONS,
MARK AND JEFF, WHO TAUGHT ME ALL I KNOW ABOUT PLAY.

ALL PHOTOGRAPHS BY M. PAUL FRIEDBERG EXCEPT PAGES
4, 64, 72, 84 & 123. THESE PHOTOS TAKEN BY RON GREEN
OF GRAPHICS 3, PORTLAND, OREGON.

TABLE OF CONTENTS

ABBREVIATIONS AND NOTES:

CONC. - CONCRETE
DIA - DIAMETER
LAG BOLT - COACH SCREW
LEACHING RING - SOAKAWAY
HOMOSOTE - INSULATION BOARD
STYROFOAM - FOAM POLYSTYRENE
RAILROAD TIE - SLEEPER
IMPERIAL TO METRIC CONVERSION TABLE APPEARS ON PAGE 123

FOREWORD

DO IT YOURSELF PLAYGROUNDS IS A SKETCHBOOK OF DESIGNS BASED ON TWO VERY SIMPLE PREMISES: ANYONE CAN BUILD A PLAYGROUND, AND THE ACTUAL PROCESS OF BUILDING IT CAN BE AS IMPORTANT AS THE FINISHED PRODUCT. IT GIVES THE BUILDERS (WHO SHOULD CERTAINLY INCLUDE THE CHILDREN FOR WHOM IT IS PLANNED) A CHANCE TO SHAPE THEIR ENVIRONMENT, TO CREATE SOMETHING TO ANSWER THEIR SPECIFIC NEEDS.

I HAVE TRIED TO PROVIDE AS WIDE A RANGE OF DESIGNS AS POSSIBLE, FROM THE SIMPLEST, LIKE THE TIRE SWING, WHICH REQUIRES ONLY THE KNOT TYING OF ROPES OR CABLES, TO FAIRLY COMPLEX WOOD STRUCTURES, WHICH CALL FOR POWER TOOLS SUCH AS DRILLS, SABER SAWS, ETC. AND I HAVE INCLUDED ENOUGH TECHNICAL INFORMATION SO THAT THE SKETCHES CAN BE FOLLOWED LITERALLY OR CAN SERVE AS POINTS OF DEPARTURE FOR THE READER'S OWN SKILLS AND PREFERENCES. WHATEVER YOUR EXPERTISE WITH TOOLS, THERE ARE PLAYGROUND DESIGNS TO MATCH IT.

ALL SETTINGS, URBAN, SUBURBAN AND RURAL, ARE RICH IN
NATURAL AND MAN-MADE MATERIALS SUITABLE FOR PLAY.
EVERY CHILD, WHEREVER HE OR SHE LIVES AND WHATEVER
SPACE IS AVAILABLE, CAN HAVE AN EXCITING PLAYGROUND.
ALL IT TAKES IS A LITTLE IMAGINATION.

IN THIS BOOK I HAVE ARBITRARILY SELECTED MATERIALS
THAT CAN BE EASILY FOUND OR INEXPENSIVELY PURCHASED,
SUCH AS BARRELS, LADDERS, CANS, LUMBER, OLD TIRES,
BOTH TO SHOW THE POTENTIALITIES INHERENT IN
READILY AVAILABLE OBJECTS AND TO UNDERLINE THE
POINT THAT BUILDING A PLAYGROUND NEED NOT TAKE
A GREAT DEAL OF MONEY. BY REARRANGING,
MODIFYING AND ADJUSTING THESE OBJECTS, YOU CAN
CREATE ENDLESS OPPORTUNITIES FOR PLAY. FOR
EXAMPLE, A CHILD IS DRAWN TO A LADDER BECAUSE
IT SUGGESTS CLIMBING, WHICH IS FUN. BY PLACING
THE LADDER IN DIFFERENT WAYS - UPRIGHT, SIDEWAYS
OR OBLIQUELY - YOU EXPAND ITS POSSIBILITIES. THE
MORE FLEXIBLE THE EQUIPMENT, THE MORE SUCCESSFUL
THE PLAYGROUND WILL BE.

INTRODUCTION

KINDS OF PLAY

OUR NOTIONS ABOUT PLAY HAVE CHANGED MARKEDLY IN THE PAST HALF-CENTURY. UNTIL LATE IN THE INDUSTRIAL REVOLUTION, CHILDREN WERE REGARDED AS MEMBERS OF THE LABOR FORCE, TO BE PRESSED INTO SERVICE AS EARLY AS POSSIBLE. THE IDEA OF CHILDHOOD AS A PERIOD OF LIFE WITH ITS OWN INTRINSIC VALUE WAS SLOW TO DEVELOP. PLAY WAS SEEN AS A NECESSARY OUTLET FOR CHILDREN, BUT ALSO AS SOMETHING TO BE DONE AS FAR AWAY AS POSSIBLE FROM THE WELL-BEHAVED ADULT WORLD. THUS THE FIRST PLAYGROUNDS WERE FENCED-IN ASPHALT SLABS SPRINKLED WITH METAL FORMS.

TODAY, HOWEVER, PSYCHOLOGISTS TELL US THAT PLAY IS AN INTEGRAL AND EXTREMELY COMPLEX PART OF A CHILD'S MENTAL, PHYSICAL AND SOCIAL GROWTH. IT CAN BE DIVIDED ROUGHLY INTO THREE MAJOR CATEGORIES: PHYSICAL PLAY, THE DEVELOPMENT OF MOTOR SKILLS; SOCIAL PLAY, THE INTERACTION BETWEEN CHILDREN; AND COGNITIVE PLAY, THE PROBLEM-SOLVING PROCESS. A PLAYGROUND SHOULD PROVIDE OPPORTUNITIES FOR ALL THREE TYPES OF PLAY.

PHYSICAL PLAY

<u>CHALLENGE AND TESTING</u>. CHILDREN ARE CONSTANTLY TESTING THEIR PHYSICAL POWERS, DISCOVERING THEIR LIMITATIONS, STRENGTHS AND PHYSICAL PROMISE. IF A PLAYGROUND DOES NOT PROVIDE SUFFICIENT CHALLENGE, THE CHILD WILL SEEK IT ELSEWHERE. THE CITY CHILD IS ALL TOO OFTEN FOUND IN THE MIDST OF THE EXCITEMENT ON A SIDEWALK OR A STREET

NEXT TO A PLAYGROUND, BECAUSE THE PLAYGROUND ITSELF IS NOT INTERESTING ENOUGH. IT IS ESSENTIAL THAT THE PLAY AREA PROVIDE EQUIPMENT THAT ALLOWS CHILDREN TO JUMP, SWING, SLIDE, CLIMB, CRAWL, RUN, FIND OUT HOW HIGH, FAR AND FAST THEY CAN GO. THE ADULT'S CAUTION TENDS TO REDUCE THE AMOUNT OF CHALLENGE BECAUSE ADULTS UNDER-ESTIMATE A CHILD'S DIS-CRETION. EVEN WHILE LEARNING THEIR CAPABILITIES, CHILDREN RARELY OVEREXTEND THEMSELVES.

AT THE SAME TIME IT IS ESSENTIAL TO TAKE INTO ACCOUNT A CHILD'S REACH, THE DISTANCE HE OR SHE CAN JUMP, CLIMB, AND SO ON, BECAUSE ALL ACTIVITIES MUST BE SCALED TO THE CHILD'S SIZE AND SKILL LEVEL. FOR EXAMPLE, A CHILD OF TWO OR THREE CAN STEP ONE FOOT HIGH AND JUMP TWO FEET. IF THE EQUIPMENT MEANT TO

CHALLENGE THREE-YEAR-OLDS REQUIRES STEPPING UP TWO FEET OR JUMPING THREE FEET, THEY ARE REALLY BEING CHALLENGED TO OVEREXTEND, FRIGHTEN, ENDANGER OR FRUSTRATE THEMSELVES. I ONCE SAW

A CLIMBING LADDER WITH PIPE RUNGS 3" IN DIAMETER, TOO THICK FOR A CHILD'S HAND TO GRASP FIRMLY. THUS A CHILD COULD NEVER FEEL FULLY CONFIDENT CLIMBING THIS LADDER.

MOST PLAY AREAS ARE INTENDED TO FUNCTION WELL FOR CHILDREN OF VARIOUS AGES WHO HAVE DIFFERENT LEVELS OF PHYSICAL DEVELOPMENT. THIS CALLS FOR A MULTIPLE SCALE, PROVIDING ALTERNATES. FOR EXAMPLE, WHEN DESIGNING STEPPING COLUMNS OR LADDERS, A VARIETY OF SIZES AND HEIGHTS SHOULD BE INCLUDED TO MEET DIVERSE ABILITIES.

SOCIAL PLAY

ROLE PLAYING. PLAY IS ALSO A TIME WHEN CHILDREN EXTEND THEMSELVES AND THEIR WORLD BEYOND THE LIMITS OF THEIR IMMEDIATE REALITY THROUGH ROLE PLAYING. A CHILD BECOMES A DOCTOR, A POLICEMAN,

A COWBOY, AN INDIAN, A DANCER. BY SUCH ROLE PLAYING, CHILDREN FIND AND TEST THE PERSONALITY CONSTRUCTS WITH WHICH THEY ARE MOST COMFORTABLE AND CARRY THEM, AS WELL AS THE ABILITY TO WORK AND PLAY WITH OTHER CHILDREN, INTO THE REAL WORLD.

TO SUPPORT THIS SIGNIFICANT PART OF PLAY, IT'S IMPORTANT TO MAKE THE PLAYGROUND AN INFORMAL STAGE WHERE THE CHILD IS ENCOURAGED TO ACT OUT VARIOUS ROLES. AN ENVIRONMENT THAT DOES NOT LITERALLY PORTRAY ONE KIND OF ACTIVITY, THAT ENCOURAGES INTERPRETATION, STIMULATES THE CHILD'S IMAGINATION. IT CAN BE MORE "REAL" TO CONVERT A HORIZONTAL LOG INTO A PLANE IN ONE'S MIND THAN TO HAVE A READY-MADE TOY PLANE PROVIDED. AND THE NEXT DAY THE LOG CAN OBLIGINGLY BECOME A SHIP OR A CAR OR A HORSE.

INTERACTION. PLAY ALLOWS CHILDREN TO DISCOVER THEMSELVES. NOT ONLY IN RELATION TO THEIR PHYSICAL SURROUNDINGS BUT ALSO IN RELATION TO EACH OTHER. I'VE DEVELOPED A VARIETY OF DIFFERENT-SIZED SPACES, FROM AN INTIMATE, SMALL ENCLOSURE, WHICH HOLDS ONLY TWO OR THREE CHILDREN, TO A GOOD-SIZED TERRITORY, WHERE SHARING IS ENCOURAGED. THESE SPACES HAVE MANY DIFFERENT FORMS. SOME ARE TOTAL ENCLOSURES WITH A WOMB-LIKE QUALITY; SOME, PLATFORMS THREE OR FOUR FEET OFF THE GROUND, WHICH ACT AS A PERCH WITH SOME OF THE QUALITIES OF A TREE HOUSE.

COOPERATION. CHILDREN DO BECOME AWARE OF SITUATIONS IN WHICH IT'S NECESSARY NOT ONLY TO INTERACT SOCIALLY BUT TO WORK TOGETHER TO A COMMON END. THE TIRE SWING, WHICH ACCOMMODATES THREE OR FOUR CHILDREN, DEMANDS A CERTAIN GIVE-AND-TAKE, WHICH THE TRADITIONAL SWING DOES NOT. IF ONE CHILD TWISTS AND ANOTHER SWINGS, CONFLICT ARISES. IN ORDER TO MAKE THE SWING WORK, COOPERATION IS NECESSARY. SIMILARLY, PORTABLE PLAY EQUIPMENT TOO HEAVY FOR ONE CHILD REQUIRES A GROUP EFFORT TO BE USED SUCCESSFULLY, TO BE PUT IN PLACE.

PROBLEM-SOLVING. A WELL-PLANNED PLAYGROUND PROVIDES A WIDE RANGE OF CHOICES, OFFERING A CHILD MANY OPPORTUNITIES TO MAKE DECISIONS AND TEST OUT THEIR CONSEQUENCES IN A CONTROLLED SITUATION. ALL PROBLEM-SOLVING HAS A CLOSE RELATIONSHIP TO CHOICES, TO DECISION-MAKING. IT IS MOST EASILY SEEN WHEN A CHILD IS PROVIDED WITH SUFFICIENT ACCESSORIES OR MATERIALS TO MAKE BASIC CHANGES IN THE PLAN OF THE PLAYGROUND. THIS IS A CREATIVE ACTIVITY WHERE THE CHILD IS SOLVING THE PROBLEMS OF PLACING LUMBER, STUDYING THE INCLINES OF SLIDES, CREATING ENCLOSURES, IN OTHER WORDS, ALTERING THE ENVIRONMENT TO PROVIDE

FOR A WIDER VARIETY OF EXPERIENCES. THEREFORE, THE RICHER THE FABRIC OF THE PLAYGROUND, THE MORE CHALLENGING THESE PROBLEMS WILL BE, AND THE MORE INNOVATIVE THE SOLUTIONS MUST BE. GIVE A CHILD THE CHOICE OF GOING OVER OR UNDER, AROUND OR THROUGH, JUMPING OR PUTTING A BRIDGE ACROSS, AND YOU ARE GIVING HIM DECISIONS TO BE MADE AND AN ENVIRONMENT TO MANIPULATE.

7

OBSERVATIONAL LEARNING.   BY BUILDING UP LEVELS
INSTEAD OF LEAVING ALL ACTIVITIES ON ONE HORIZONTAL
PLANE AS IN TRADITIONAL PLAYGROUNDS, YOU ALSO GIVE
CHILDREN OBSERVATION POINTS FOR LEARNING BY EXAMPLE.
PERCHES AND VANTAGE POINTS FOR MIXED AGE GROUPS
ARE ESPECIALLY VALUABLE. IDEALLY THE DIFFERENT
AGES AVOID PHYSICAL CONTACT, BUT INSTRUCT ONE
ANOTHER VISUALLY.

GENERAL CONSIDERATIONS   IN THE DESIGN OF PLAYGROUNDS

A PLAYGROUND IS A THREE-DIMENSIONAL SOLID. IT SHOULD
ALLOW THE CHILD TO GO UP, OVER, ACROSS AND DOWN-THE
RANGE OF EXPERIENCES THAT A CHILD ENJOYS. FOR INSTANCE.
THE CHILD BEGINS AT GROUND LEVEL, CLIMBS UP A LADDER
TO A TREEHOUSE, SWINGS ACROSS OPEN SPACE ON A TIRE, AND
RETURNS TO GROUND LEVEL VIA A SLIDE. THIS IS INFINITELY
MORE EXCITING AS A SEQUENCE OF ACTIVITIES THAN WALKING
FROM ONE OBJECT OR EVENT TO ANOTHER.
NO MATTER HOW LIMITED THE AVAILABLE RESOURCES, THERE
ARE CERTAIN WAYS OF LAYING OUT PLAYGROUNDS THAT PROVIDE
A WIDE RANGE OF POSSIBILITIES :

LINKING.   LITERALLY THIS MEANS CONNECTING THE
ELEMENTS TOGETHER. YOU CAN LINK STEPPING COLUMNS,
RAMPS, OVERLAPPING PLATFORMS, LADDERS. BY LINKING
YOU PROVIDE PATHWAYS THAT OFFER FACINATING CHOICES
AND INNUMERABLE OPTIONS. THROUGH LINKAGES, PLAY
BECOMES CONTINUOUS. IF YOU CONCEIVE OF A PLAYGROUND
AS A SINGLE ENVIRONMENT IN WHICH THE ACTIVITIES OF
SWINGING, CLIMBING AND BOUNCING ARE EXPERIENCED AS
THEY OCCUR AS ONE MOVES THROUGH THE ENVIRONMENT,
AS OPPOSED TO SEPARATING CLIMBING FROM SLIDING, ETC.,
THEN THE PLAYGROUND BECOMES A SETTING FOR
ADVENTURES.

<u>JUXTAPOSITIONING</u>. IN ADDITION TO LINKING, THERE IS THE JUXTAPOSITIONING OF PLAY ELEMENTS. PROPER JUXTAPOSITIONING AMPLIFIES AND REINFORCES THE ACTIVITY OF EACH FACILITY. FOR EXAMPLE, RUNNING DOWN A HILL DEVELOPS MOMENTUM. IF ANOTHER HILL IS JUXTAPOSED TO THE FIRST, YOU PROVIDE AN IRRESISTABLE FORCE WHICH CARRIES THE CHILD UP ONE SIDE AND DOWN THE OTHER, A RECIPROCAL, PENDULUM-LIKE ACTION. WITHOUT THE SECOND HILL, THE AMOUNT OF PLAY VALUE WOULD BE HALVED. (SPACING, OF COURSE, IS IMPORTANT: IF THE SECOND HILL IS TOO FAR AWAY THE MOMENTUM FROM THE FIRST IS LOST.) WHEN A CHILD SLIDES, HE SHOULD LAND AT THE BEGINING OF A PATH. MOREOVER, IF A PLAYGROUND HAS A HILL, BUILD A SLIDE INTO IT, MAKING THE CLIMB UP AND THE SLIDE DOWN A MORE ORGANIC RELATIONSHIP.

EACH FACILITY SHOULD BE MULTI- USE AND MULTI- PURPOSE. FOR EXAMPLE, MANY OF THE PLAY FACILITIES CAN BE USED AS LINKS AS WELL AS FOR SPECIFIC ACTIVITIES. A LADDER CAN LINK A MOUND TO A TREEHOUSE AND BE CONVERTED IN TURN INTO A SUPERSTRUCTURE FROM WHICH A SWING CAN BE HUNG. THE SUPERSTRUCTURE HAS AS MUCH PLAY VALUE AS THE SWING OR LADDER BY THEMSELVES. THE SAME STRUCTURE COULD BE DRAPED WITH CANVAS AND CONVERTED INTO AN ENCLOSURE. AN ELEVATED PLATFORM SO COVERED BECOMES A TREEHOUSE. TIMBERS OR LOGS CAN BE USED AS STEPPING LINKS OR FOR BALANCING OR STRADDLING. PLATFORMS CAN BE GROUPED TO CREATE AN INFORMAL THEATER. THE POSSIBILITIES HERE ARE TRULY BOUNDLESS.

THE EXCITEMENT AND USE OF A PLAYGROUND SHOULD LAST FOR YEARS, IF IT IS PLANNED FOR ADAPTABILITY AND

9

FLEXIBILITY. A CHILD EXHAUSTS THE LIMITS OF THE PLAYGROUND THAT CAN'T CHANGE WITH HIS CHANGING SKILLS, SIZE AND KNOWLEDGE. BEYOND THE PREDETERMINED ACCESSORIES. SUCH AS PLANKS, LADDERS, ADDITIONAL TIRES, THE PLAY-GROUND SHOULD READILY ACCEPT MATERIALS SUCH AS STYROFOAM, CARDBOARD, HOMOSOTE, ROPES AND STRING FOR MACRAMÉ, AND PAPER MACHÉ. YEARS OF INTEREST, STIMULATION AND ENJOYMENT CAN BE ADDED TO THE PLAYGROUND. MOREOVER, AS THE CHILD GROWS OLDER, THE ADDITION OF COMPONENTS THAT CHALLENGE INCREASED PHYSICAL SIZE AND STRENGTH AND ALLOW FOR CHANGES IN INTEREST IS ONE WAY TO ASSURE CONTINUED INTENSIVE USE OF THE PLAYGROUND. PLAYGROUNDS CAN BE CONSTANTLY REPLENISHED AND REINVIGORATED WITH IMAGINATION.

SCALE

ACTIVITIES MATRIX

○ PARTIAL
● TOTAL

	RINGS/HOOPS	SEE SAW	TIRE SWING	LADDERS	BRIDGES	RAMPS	SPRING PADS	CANVAS PANEL	WATER	TIRES	55 GAL. DRUMS	CLIMBER	SAND	ROLLER	BALANCE BEAM	NET	SLIDE	SLIDE POLE
PHYSICAL																		
CLIMBING				●		○				○	●	●				●		
SLIDING																	●	●
HANGING	●		○		○			○		○	○	●						
JUMPING						○	●		○	○	○	○	●			○		
SWINGING	○		●						●							○		
CRAWLING				●	○	○				●	●		○					
HIDING										○	○							
BALANCING		●	●	○			●				●	○		●	●			
SOCIAL																		
INTERACTION	○	●	●	○	○		●	●	●	○	○	○	○	●	●	○		
PARTICIPATION	○	●	●	○	○	○	●	○	●	●	●	○	●	○	○	●	○	○
ROLE PLAYING	○	○	○	○	○	○	○	○	●	●	●	○	●	○	○	●	●	●
COOPERATION		●	●		○	○	●		○	○		●				●	●	
COGNITIVE																		
MANIPULATION	○	○	○					○	○	○			○	○	○			
PROBLEM SOLVING		○		●	○	○			●	●	●		●	○	○	○		
CHOOSING	○			○	○	○				○	○	○	○		○			
INTERPRETATION	●		○	○				○	●	●	●		●			●		
GENERAL																		
FLEXIBILITY	○		○	○					●	●	○		●			●		
LINKAGES	○			●	●	●	○	●	○	○	●		○		○	●	○	○
RESPONSIVENESS	○	●	●				●	○	●	○			●	○		○		

LADDERS

3×12 PLANK

PLATFORM

3'-0"

12"

12"

ADJ. ANGLE

HOLES

ACCESS

3/4" ROPE RAIL
AS DESIRED

STANDARD
RUNG LADDER

4x4 BRACE

3/4" MARINE
PLYWOOD
PLATFORM

4" — RAIL
DEPTH

PROVIDE POSTS
AS REQUIRED.
CANTILEVERS
NOT TO EXCEED
3'-0"

6x6 POSTS
3'-0" BELOW GROUND
IN CONC. FOOTING

• LADDERS ARE PREFABRICATED
  MODULAR UNITS (WOOD OR ALUMINUM).
  TAKE CARE NOT TO CREATE SPANS
  THAT EXCEED LADDER STRENGTH.
  A GOOD RULE-OF-THUMB IS SPAN 2'
  FOR EVERY INCH OF RAIL DEPTH.
  A 4" RAIL WILL SPAN 8'-0".

14

4x12's

14' MIN.

EYE BOLT

⅜" CHAIN

MAIN SUPPORTS
TO BE 3-4'
BELOW GRADE

CLATTER BRIDGE
MAX. SPAN 12-14'

12" DIAM. LOGS
OR UTILITY POLES
BOLTED TOGETHER

EYE BOLT

FILL VOIDS WITH
I PART CEMENT
3 PARTS SAND so
FEET DON'T GET
CAUGHT

PLAN

POLES

CUT POLE TOPS ON A 45° ANGLE

SUPPORT- 3-4' BELOW GROUND.

ON GROUND

ABOVE GROUND

PLAN

RECESS BOLT

NUT

WASHER

MACHINE BOLT

4×12's

EYE BOLT

8'-0" MIN.

MAIN SUPPORTING
MEMBERS TO BE
4'-0" BELOW GROUND
IN CONC. FOOTINGS

TIRE SWING

LOG ROLLER

● IF POLES ARE AVAILABLE THEY
MAKE EXCELLENT PLAYFORMS. THE
WEIGHT OF THE GROUPINGS REQUIRES THAT ONLY
THE TALLEST POLES HAVE FOOTINGS
SINCE THEY'RE USED TO SUPPORT
SWINGS & LADDERS.

MAX. POLE
LENGTH 12'

COUNTERSINK
WASHER & NUT

BURY LOGS
3'-0" BELOW
GROUND.

BALANCING
POLES

EYE BOLT

EYE BOLT

POLES AND DOWELS

SET DOWELS WITH NAIL

LADDER

ROPE OR CHAIN

CUT POLE ENDS ON ANGLE

PLATFORM
2×8 SPAN 4'
3×8 " 6'
4×8 " 8'

ROUND DOWEL
EDGE

LADDER
MAX. HT. 8'

1'-0"

1½" DIA.
WOOD OR PIPE

NOTCH
POLE

USE METAL
STRAP IF LOG
SPLITS

SPAN
6" DIA. - 8'
8" DIA. - 10'
10" DIA. - 12'

6"-10" DIA.
LOG OR POLE

OTHER ACCESSORIES CAN BE ADDED
TO THIS SYSTEM

20

PLATFORM 1" MARINE PLYWOOD

1½" DIA. WOOD OR PIPE

SADDLE CLAMP

MAX. 5'-0"

60°

PLAN

BURY POLES
2-3' BELOW
GROUND.

TIMBERFORM - PORTLAND, OREGON

SLIDE POLE

ADD ON OTHER ACCESSORIES AS DESIRED

LINK TO ANOTHER GROUPING

BRIDGE

IF PIPE IS USED, PLUG ENDS WITH WOOD DOWEL

ROPE CONNECTION

ROPE RAIL

BOLT CONNECTION

BURY SUPPORTING LOGS 3' BELOW GROUND.

PLAN

23

LOGS

PLAN

24

2-8" DIA. LOGS

8'-0" MIN.

PLANK BRIDGE 4×8's

SUPPORTING MEMBERS 4' BELOW GROUND.

RAMP

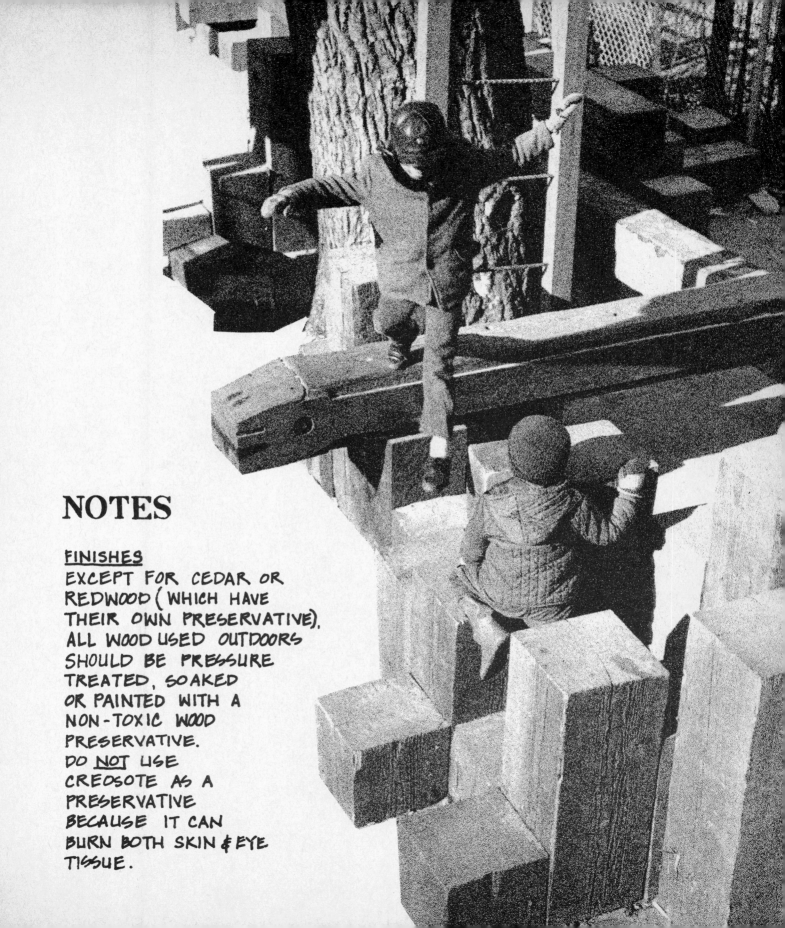

NOTES

FINISHES
EXCEPT FOR CEDAR OR
REDWOOD (WHICH HAVE
THEIR OWN PRESERVATIVE),
ALL WOOD USED OUTDOORS
SHOULD BE PRESSURE
TREATED, SOAKED
OR PAINTED WITH A
NON-TOXIC WOOD
PRESERVATIVE.
DO **NOT** USE
CREOSOTE AS A
PRESERVATIVE
BECAUSE IT CAN
BURN BOTH SKIN & EYE
TISSUE.

STEPPING COLUMNS

2" DIA. PIPE

BURY BELOW GROUND.

LAG BOLT PIECES TOGETHER

BURY 3'-0" BELOW GROUND.

DRILL HOLE

4x12 PLANK SPAN 8'-0"

RINGS LASHED
TO ROPE

SLACK IN ROPE
IS ADJUSTABLE -
LOOP END

1½" DIA.
WOOD DOWEL

SLIDE POLE

4" DIA.
BALANCE PIPE

TOP EDGES TO
BE CHAMFERED

6×6
8×8
10×10
12×12

LAG BOLT
STEPPING COLUMNS
TOGETHER

8'-0" MIN.

12 x 12's

6'-0"

2'-0"

BURY BELOW GROUND.

LAG SCREW
TIMBERS TOGETHER.

HOLE OR
COUNTERSINK

1½" DIA. WOOD
DOWEL

PLAN

POST AND CHAIN

THE POST & CHAIN
SYSTEM OFFERS
OPPORTUNITIES FOR
BALANCE AND
COORDINATION.

12×12 OR
8×8

ADD TO THIS FRAME ANY
ACCESSORIES YOU DESIRE
(NETS, BRIDGES, PLATFORMS ETC.)

CHAIN

LAG BOLT

6×6 OR
4×4

BURY TIMBERS
BELOW GROUND

SCREW EYE

6"

6"

½ CHAIN

2×4 BEAM

1½" DIA. WOOD DOWEL

2×8's FOR PLATFORM

6×6

BURY 3'-0" BELOW GROUND

32

3'

8"

6'

3'

3'

6'

3'

POSTS CAN BE
4x4 6x6 OR 8x8

8"-16"

PLATFORM PIECES
3x4 3x6 3x8 3x12
MAX. SPAN 6'0"

SADDLE CLAMP

1½" DIA. PIPE OR
WOOD DOWEL

33

POST AND DOWEL

BRIDGE : LINK
TO OTHER PLAY AREAS

SHACKLE
CONNECTION

4'x4' MARINE PLYWOOD
PLAQUE 3/4" THICKNESS

DRILLED TIMBERS
CAN BE PLACED
HORIZONTALLY &
VERTICALLY

BURY POSTS
BELOW GROUND

• THESE ARE BASICALLY SIMILAR
TO POLE & DOWEL SYSTEMS,
EXCEPT THAT THEY ARE
EASIER TO WORK WITH &
OFFER AN ENORMOUS
RANGE OF POTENTIAL
ACTIVITIES & DIVERSE
PLACEMENTS.

SLIDE POLE

SLIDE

PLAN

35

PLAN

TIRE SWING

CLUSTER OF
6x6, 8x8 OR
12x12

36

MAX. SPANS
4×4 — 8'
6×6 — 10'
8×8 — 14'

PLATFORM

¾" DIA. EYE BOLT

LINK

LINK TO
OTHER CLUSTER

PLAN

TIRE SWING
STRUCTURE
SHOULD BE
SUNK 4' BELOW
GROUND

37

NOTES

BOTH THE SIDES AND TOPS OF ALL WOOD EDGES SHOULD BE CHAMFERED OR ROUNDED A MIN. OF ¼", AND SOMETIMES AS MUCH AS 1". SAND ALL ROUGH SPOTS AND ELIMINATE ALL LARGE SPLINTERED AREAS.

WOOD WILL CONTINUE TO CHECK AND SHRINK, BUT AS LONG AS THERE ARE NO MAJOR SPLINTER AREAS, CHILDREN WILL DEVELOP A SENSE OF DISCRETION AND USE CAUTION.

SLIDE POLE

1½" WOOD DOWEL

4x12 PLANK
SPAN 3'-0"

2x12 12' LONG

DOOR PULL OR
ROPE HANDLE

• THIS ARCHITECTONIC PLAY ENVIRONMENT
IS EASILY ASSEMBLED WITH PRECUT
LUMBER.

4×4 BEAM

BURY EVERY THIRD OR FOURTH PIECE 3'-0" BELOW GROUND.

NAIL THRU DOWEL TO KEEP FROM TURNING

1½" DIA. WOOD DOWEL

USE 4×4, 4×6 OR 4×8's LAG BOLT PIECES TOGETHER

40

PIPE CAP

SET SCREW FOR TOP MEMBER

WASHER

2½" DIA. PIPE FOR SPACER

2" DIA. PIPE FOR STRUCTURE

4×6

2½" DIA. PIPE RESTS ON CONC. FOOTING

CONC. FOOTING 2'×2'×2'

2" DIA. PIPE IN CONC. FOOTING

6' MAX.

PLATFORM OF 4×6's

4×6
4×8
4×12

PIPE CAPS

PLAN

ALTERNATE MEANS OF SUPPORT - SCREW DIRECTLY INTO PIPE THRU TIMBER

POST AND PIPE

EYE BOLT

ROPE RAIL AS REQ'D.

PIPE CAPS

PLATFORM

4×6

1½" DIA. WOOD OR PIPE

CAP NUT

PLATFORM

SECTION

4×6

- THIS SYSTEM IS FLEXIBLE. IF THE PIPES ARE PUT ON A MODULE, THE WOOD CROSS MEMBERS CAN BE REARRANGED. IF RAIL ROAD TIES ARE USED, BE SURE THEY ARE NOT COVERED WITH CREOSOTE.

8' MIN.

BOLTS

2- 4×12's

EYE BOLT

12"

8" DIA. LOG OR POLE BOLTED TO WATER TANKS

2" DIA. WOOD DOWELS TO SUPPORT PLATFORMS

LADDER RUNGS

BURY POLES 4' BELOW GROUND

LADDER

4×12 PLANK

2×6 PLATFORM NAILED TO 2" DIA. WOOD DOWEL.

43

CLAMP

TENSION
RINGS

PLANK

STEEL
ANGLE

BOLT TANKS
TOGETHER

3x12 RAMP

CUT OPENINGS IN TANKS

FILL WITH SAND
OR WATER

WATER TANKS

44

PLATFORM
3×6's SCREWED
TO RAILS.

MOVEABLE
PLATFORM PIECES

TREEHOUSE OF
1" MARINE PLYWOOD
SCREWED TO FENCE
RAILS.

CUT OPENINGS
IN TREEHOUSE
SIDES.

NAIL THRU
POST INTO
RAIL

RAILS NOT TO
EXCEED 8' SPAN

BURY FENCE
POSTS 18-24"
BELOW GROUND

FENCE

HALF-ROUND MOULDING 1" RADIUS OR 1×2's SCREWED INTO 2×6's

2×6 RAMP

FOR ADDITIONAL HT. STRAP OR BOLT TWO FENCE POSTS TOGETHER

FENCE RAIL

2×12

CARRAGE BOLT

4×4 WOOD BLOCKING

SLIDE POLE

6×6 POST

2×6

STOCKADE
FENCE

RAMP

3'-0"

5'-0"

PLATFORM

2×6

2×10

6×6

2×6

BURY 6×6 3'-0"
BELOW GROUND INTO
1'×1'×1' CONC. FOOTING

47

• FENCING PROVIDES A PLAY AREA AT MINIMAL COST. STOCKADE FENCE SYSTEMS STIMULATE FANTASIES ASSOCIATED WITH OLD FORTS.

6 x 6 POSTS

4 x 12 PLANKS

STOCKADE FENCE

BRIDGE

SLIDE POLE

SLIDE

RAMP

PLAN

ROPE NET

6 x 6 STAKE

STACKED TIMBERS

2-6x6's

WOOD FOOTING

5'

PROJECT BOTTOM MEMBER OUT ±5' AND BURY BELOW GROUND.

SADDLE CLAMP

2" DIA. PIPE

EYE BOLT

COUNTERSINK
WASHER & NUT

⅝" DIA. PIPE
WITH THREADED
ENDS

BRIDGE

BOLT PIECES
TOGETHER

CONNECTOR PLATE
TO AVOID WOOD
MEMBERS ROTATING

2×4, 3×4 OR 4×6

3¾" MARINE
PLYWOOD

BURY LEGS 1'-0"

LINK TO ANOTHER STRUCTURE

PROVIDE OPENINGS WHERE POSSIBLE

SLIDE POLE

2-4×12

BRIDGE

4'

6×6 POSTS BOLTED TO STRUCTURE & BURIED 3'-0"

STACKED TIMBERS ARE MADE FROM 2×4's, 3×4's, 4×6's -
THE SIZE DEPENDS UPON THE DESIRED SCALE. THE
LARGER MEMBERS ARE RECOMMENDED FOR INSTITUTIONAL
USE.

THIS IS ESSENTIALLY A VERY SIMPLE SYSTEM IN WHICH
EACH ELEMENT CAN BE HELD TOGETHER BY A CONTINUOUS
PIPE, OR ONE CROSSMEMBER CAN BE LAG BOLTED INTO
THE OTHERS. RACKING CAN BE A PROBLEM AND PREVENT-
ATIVE MEASURES SHOULD BE TAKEN. USING METAL
BRACES, NOTCHING EACH PIECE INTO THE OTHERS, OR
DOUBLE BOLTING ARE ALL SOLUTIONS.

THESE STRUCTURES ARE STURDY AND REQUIRE NO
FOOTINGS EXCEPT IN CASES WHERE THE TOP
IS GREATER THAN THE BOTTOM. IN THESE
SITUATIONS THE BOTTOM RAIL SHOULD BE
MADE THE SAME LENGTH AS THE TOP AND
PLACED BELOW GRADE.

2×4

4×4

1'-0"

ROUND
ENDS

$3\frac{1}{2}$" $1\frac{1}{2}$" $3\frac{1}{2}$"

6"

$1\frac{1}{2}$" WOOD DOWEL 19" LONG

$1\frac{1}{2}$" WOOD DOWEL 6'-5" LONG

2×8

6" 5" 4'-7" 5" 6"

$3\frac{1}{2}$" 4'-7" $3\frac{1}{2}$"

53

PLATFORM
3×8 PIECES

SLIDE

5'-0" o.c.

5'-0"
o.c.

PLAN

BOLT

LINK TO
ANOTHER CLUSTER

BURY TALL
COLUMNS 3'
SHORT ONES
BURY 2'

CLUSTERS

54

EARTH WORK

3'-0"
2'-0"
CHAIN RAIL
3×6 DECK
12×12 POSTS
4×12 BEAM
BURY 4'-0"
16' MAXIMUM

PROVIDE TEXTURED
SURFACE TO
FACILITATE
CLIMBING
1½"

SLIDE BUILT INTO
A HILL

GRANITE BLOCK
OR LARGE STONES SHOULD BE
USED WHERE SLOPE IS
1:3 OR GREATER. MAX. SLOPE
SHOULD NOT EXCEED 1:1

1
3
SLOPE

6' ON CENTER

8×8 POST
1½" PIPE
3×12 MOVEABLE
PLANK
WOOD BLOCKING

CARGO NET

MOUND

SLIDE

TREE HOUSE

BRIDGE

CONSTRUCTION AREA

STEPPING COLUMNS

EARTH CONTOURS

CABLE RIDE

TUNNEL

VARIES

SECTION

CONC. PIPE

3'-0" MIN.

END VIEW

NETS

ROPE SNAP HOOK

1½" WOOD DOWELS LACED TO ROPE

2'-0

ROUND ENDS OF DOWELS

¾" MARINE PLYWOOD

PLATFORM

2x4 FRAME   SCREW HOOKS

BRAIDED END

LASHED END   SNAP HOOK

CARGO NET   BRAIDED LOOPS

PLANK W/HOOKS
2x12 4'-0" LONG
3x12 6'-0" "

BASE PLATE

CLAMP

SECOND LEVEL

STACKING PIN

PLYWOOD PLAQUES

ROPE LADDER

3x12 PLANK

SLIDE POLE

CONC. FOOTING

PLYWOOD
PANELS TAILOR
THE SYSTEM
TO INDIVIDUAL
TASTE & SCALE.

SCAFFOLDING

TREE HOUSE

• ONE OF THE MOST MEANINGFUL PLAY FORMS, A TREE HOUSE PROVIDES CHILDREN WITH A SENSE OF OWNERSHIP AND STIMULATES IMAGINATION AND FANTASY. DO NOT BE AFRAID TO BOLT THROUGH A TREE. PROPER DRILLING AND WOUND TREATMENTS ELIMINATE THE POSSIBILITY OF THE TREE DYING. I DO RECOMMEND, FOR SAFETY, THAT ROPE RAILINGS BE USED.

EYE BOLT

LAG BOLT

ROPE RAIL

2×6 DECK SPAN 4'-0"

2-2×4's SPAN 6'-0"

NOTES

IF COLOR IS DESIRED, INSTEAD OF
PAINT USE A WOOD STAIN; IT
REQUIRES LESS MAINTENANCE
AND WEATHERS BETTER.

DRUMS

STANDARD 55 GAL. OIL DRUM

BOLT TOGETHER

CUT OUT STEPS

FLANGE

2" DIA. PIPE

2' BELOW GROUND

PAINT ON GRAPHICS

ROLLING DRUM

65

- WHEN AVAILABLE, THESE VERSATILE DRUMS CAN BE USED FOR ENCLOSURES, TUNNELS AND PLATFORMS. THE FOLLOWING PAGES ILLUSTRATE DESIGNS COMBINING DRUMS WITH OTHER ELEMENTS AND SYSTEMS.

GARDEN HOSE

METAL DRUM

SLIDE POLE

PLANK

PLAN

PLANK

CUT-OUTS AS DESIRED

USE CARRAGE BOLT
AND CAP NUT TO
AVOID SKIN CUTS

2×6

4×4 OR
6×6

1½" WOOD DOWEL
OR PIPE

BURY 3'-0"

HALF DRUM

CUT OUTS

METAL DRUM

CARRAGE BOLT

NUT OR CAP NUT

2×6

4×4
BRACE

END DRUMS
REST ON GROUND

2-2×6

BURY 3' BELOW GROUND
IN CONC. FOOTING

GARDEN HOSE

METAL DRUM

68

5/8" DIA. PIPE

PIPE LADDER

LINK TO ANOTHER PLAY STRUCTURE

2'×2'×2' CONC. FOOTING 3' BELOW GR.

CAP NUT OPTIONAL

2½" DIA. PIPE STRUCTURE

DRUMS BOLTED TOGETHER & BOLTED TO PIPE

2" DIA. PIPE WITH ELBOWS

EYE BOLT

PIPE 2½" DIA.

LACED END OR
CABLE CLAMP

EYE BOLT

8x8

SLIDE POLE

3x10 PLANK
MAX. SPAN
6'-0"

ROUND HEAD SCREW

TUBES

¾" MARINE PLYWOOD

TIRE TUBES

ELASTIC ROPE

ALTERNATE: TUBES CAN ALSO SUPPORT PLYWOOD AT INTERSECTIONS

PLAN

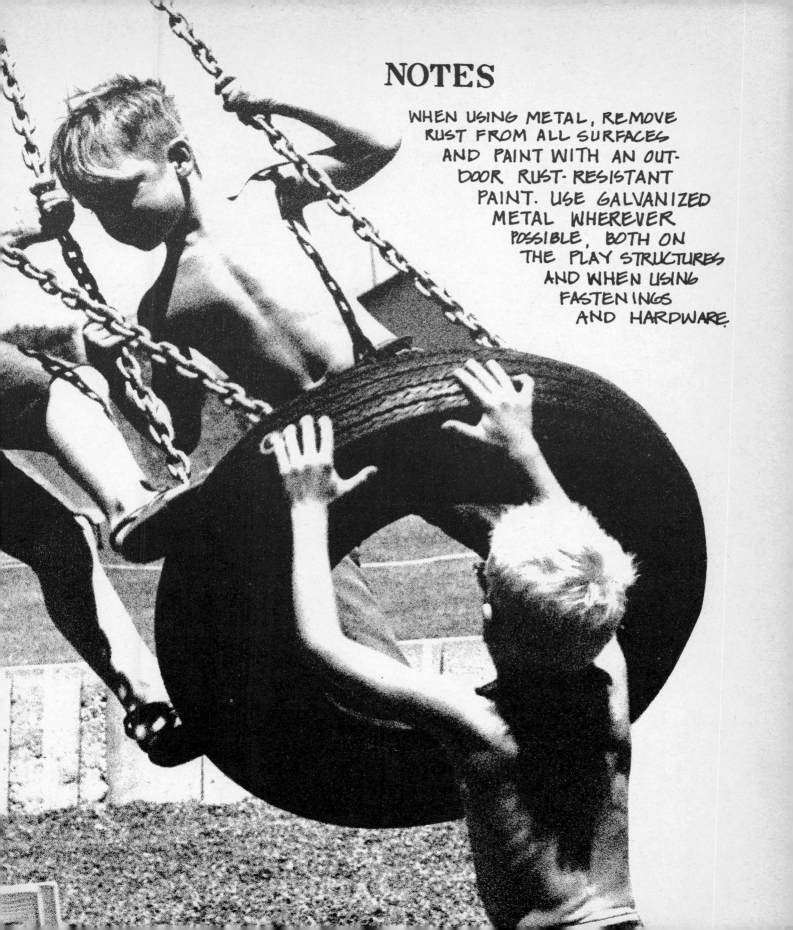

NOTES

WHEN USING METAL, REMOVE
RUST FROM ALL SURFACES
AND PAINT WITH AN OUT-
DOOR RUST-RESISTANT
PAINT. USE GALVANIZED
METAL WHEREVER
POSSIBLE, BOTH ON
THE PLAY STRUCTURES
AND WHEN USING
FASTENINGS
AND HARDWARE.

TIRES

EYE BOLT

ROPE

EYE BOLT

KNOT INSIDE TIRE

10" DIA. POLE OR
4" DIA PIPE
BURY 4'-0" BELOW
IN CONC. FOOTING

• TIRES ARE HIGHLY RECOMMENDED;
THEY ARE READILY AVAILABLE, SAFE
AND CAN BE PUT TO MANY USES.
HERE ARE ILLUSTRATIONS OF HOW
TIRES CAN BE ARRANGED TO CREATE VARIETY.

POST

TIRES BOLTED TOGETHER

HANG FROM TREE OR PLAY STRUCTURE

TIRE SWING

BOLT CONNECTION

TIRES IN VERTICAL & HORIZONTAL POSITIONS

74

½" DIA. CHAIN

EYE BOLT

WOOD BLOCKING INSIDE TIRE

TIRES CHAINED OR BOLTED TOGETHER

TIRES BOLTED TO PIPE

10" DIA. POLE (6x6 OR 8x8) BURIED 3' BELOW GR. IN CONC. FOOTING

2" DIA. PIPE 3' BELOW GROUND IN CONC. FOOTING

POST

PLAN

USE A VARIETY
OF TIRE SIZES

SCREW EYE

WOOD BLOCKING
INSIDE TIRE

$\frac{1}{2}$" CHAIN

BURY $\frac{1}{2}$ BELOW
GROUND

76

SPOOLS

TOE NAIL 3×12
PLANK IN PLACE

BOLT SPOOLS
TOGETHER

BURY 6" IN
GROUND

ANCHOR BOLT
BOTTOM SPOOL
TO CONC.
FOOTING

BURY POST 2'

PLYWOOD

6×6

NAIL DOWEL
IN PLACE

2" DIA.
WOOD
DOWEL

STEP 1: FLATTEN ENDS

ALUMINUM PIPE

STEP 2: BEND ENDS TO REQUIRED ANGLE

3/4" MARINE PLYWOOD DISC 6" DIA.

• THESE CLIMBING DOMES MAKE PROTECTIVE ENCLOSURES FOR SWINGS, LADDERS AND SLIDES AND CAN BE PLACED OVER SAND.

PIPE STRUT

PLYWOOD CONNECTOR

GEODESIC DOME

CONC. PIPE

3" DIA. PIPE

PLAN

DETAIL SHOWING HOW TO STACK CONC. PIPES SO THAT THE TOP ONE CAN'T BE MOVED

PRECAST CONC. CAP

PRECAST CONC. PIPE SECTIONS

3' DIA.

4'-0"

DOME TOP FOR PRECAST CONC. LEACHING RING 3'-8' IN DIAM

4' TO 8'

3' TO 4'

PRECAST CONC. LEACHING RING

8' DIAM.

SECTION

CONCRETE PIPE AND RINGS

PRECAST STRUCTURES ARE VERY DURABLE BUT AVAILABLE ONLY IN CERTAIN PARTS OF THE COUNTRY, SOMETIMES AS SECONDS AT A MODERATE PRICE. IT IS RECOMMENDED THAT A MASONRY FILE OR STONE BE USED TO SMOOTH ROUGH CONCRETE SPOTS. THE HOLES CAN BE USED FOR SETTING PLATFORMS AND PIPES AND CLIMBING.

4 X 8

CHAIN SHACKLE

1½" DIA. PIPE

3" DIA. PIPE TO SUPPORT PLATFORM

4'

THREADED FLANGE

FILL IN WITH MORTAR

PIPE

NOTCH ENDS OF PLATFORM
PIECES TO MATCH OPENINGS
IN BLOCKS.

BLOCKS CAN BE STACKED
IN A VARIETY OF WAYS
TO ADD TEXTURE &
FACILITATE CLIMBING

BLOCKS SET
VERTICALLY

AMPHITHEATER

CONCRETE BLOCK

3×8's PLATFORM

BEAM

SLIDE

3×6 OR 3×8 PLANK
SPAN 6'-0"

USE MASONRY
NAILS TO ANCHOR
WOOD TO CONC. BLOCK

82

MORTAR
BETWEEN BLOCKS

CONC. BLOCK

START WALL SEVERAL
COURSES BELOW GROUND

CONC.
FOOTING

PROVIDE
"DUR-O-WALL"
BETWEEN COURSES
OF BLOCK

2" DIA. WOOD
OR PIPE

1½" DIA. WOOD
DOWELS LACED
TO ¾" ROPE

NOTES

FOOTINGS GENERALLY SHOULD BE PLACED BELOW THE FROST LINE OR SHOULD BE OF SUFFICIENT DEPTH TO PREVENT RACKING OR FAILURE. UNLESS THERE ARE PROPER FOOTINGS POLES, WHICH SUPPORT SWINGS OR LADDERS, CAN BEGIN TO SWAY AT THE TOP.

THE BEST PAVEMENTS TO USE ARE SOFT NATURAL MATERIALS THAT HAVE PLAY VALUE AND PROVIDE PROTECTION, LIKE SAND, WELL-DRAINED EARTH OR TANBARK. ONE OF THE DIFFICULTIES IN USING NATURAL MATERIALS IN HIGH DENSITY AREAS IS THE PROBLEM OF GERMS, DOGS AND MUD. THEREFORE, WHEN IT IS NOT FEASIBLE TO USE NATURAL MATERIALS, I WOULD RECOMMEND SOME OF THE COMMERCIALLY MANUFACTURED RESILIENT PAVEMENTS SUCH AS RUBBER MATS OR RESILIENT ASPHALT PAVEMENT

ACCESSORIES

THESE CAN BE
6×6, 8×8, 10×10
OR 12×12

- <u>ACCESSORIES</u>
THE FOLLOWING COMPONENTS
ARE ACCESSORIES THAT
SUPPORT PLAYGROUND
ACTIVITIES SUCH AS SWINGS,
SLIDES, BIKE RACKS, ETC.

COLUMN CAPITALS

CABLE AND PIPE SLIDE

PIPE CAP

BANNER

3" DIA. PIPE

SLIDE POLE

TIRE CUSHION

BURY 4' BELOW GR. IN 2'×2'×2' CONC. FOOTING

TURNBUCKLE

3" DIA. PIPE

SET SCREW

CABLE RIDE

TURNBUCKLE

PULLEY OR STEEL RING

12×12 POST

EYE BOLT

ROPE

PLATFORM

GROUND

BURY 4' MIN

86

PLATFORM

2×4

2×4

STAINLESS STEEL

BOLT TOGETHER

PLATFORM

BENT METAL BRACKET

SCORE 3/4" PLYWOOD

WOOD BLOCKING

2" DIA. PIPE 2' BELOW GROUND IN CONC. FOOTING

SADDLE CLAMP

CUT RAILS FROM 2×12

CONC. FTG.

STAINLESS ST.

CUT FROM 2×10

BOLT HALVES
TOGETHER

STAINLESS STEEL
ON ¾" EXTERIOR
PLYWOOD

2×4

SLIDES

½" ROPE 2

¾" " 2

1" " 2

KNOT

MARINE
BUOYS CAN
ALSO BE USED

SECTIONS
OF WOOD
POST

FOAM
BALL (BUOY)

2'-0"

1" MARINE
PLYWOOD

KNOT

12"

1" MARINE
PLYWOOD SEAT

24"

2 x 12

2'-0"

12"

5"

SWINGS

STEEL RING

SWIVEL

STEEL RING

CABLE

CABLE CLAMP

½" CHAIN

EYE BOLT

WOOD BLOCKING TO KEEP TIRE FROM CRUSHING

LASHED ENDS

TIRE

STEEL RING TO FIT IN TIRE

BENT METAL PLATE EYE BOLTS

ROPE.

3×12

2×2

BY MOVING THE SEESAW DOWN A NOTCH A HEAVY AND A LIGHT CHILD CAN BALANCE.

MAX. LENGTH 8'

ROPE HANDLE

3×12

2×2

END VIEW

8×8 OR 12×12

PIPE AT VARIOUS LEVELS TO ACCOMMODATE CHILDREN OF DIFFERENT SIZES

GR.

BURY 3'

TIRE BURIED ¾ BELOW GR. FOR HEEL CUSHION IF DESIRED.

SEESAWS

2×6

2×10

1½" WOOD DOWEL

2×10

8×8 OR 12×12

BOLT PIECES
TOGETHER

18-24"

BURY 3'

BENT METAL
A DOOR PULL MAY BE
USED FOR A HANDLE

ALTERNATE
HANDLE

2½" DIA. PIPE

BOLT PIECES TOGETHER

SADDLE CLAMP

2×12

3×12

HALF ROUND MOULDING

4×12 BRIDGE
MAX. SPAN 8'-0"

MAX. LENGTH 8'

1½" DIA. PIPE

SADDLE CLAMP

2×4

4×6

BOLT PIECES TOGETHER W/ THREADED ROD

2×12 OR 1" PLYWOOD SCREWED TO 2-2×4's MAX. SPAN 8'-0"

2×4

STANDARD
RUNG LADDER

4×8

8"

12"-18"

ROUND OFF
DOWEL ENDS

STEEL
RING

18"-24"

BENT METAL
CLIP

2'-0"

¾" ROPE WITH STEEL
RINGS LASHED ON

MAX. SPAN 10'-0"

4x8's

1/2" CHAIN

2'-0"

6x6's

EYE BOLT

6x6

SCREW EYE

3x12 OR
4x12 RAMP

HALF ROUND
MOULDING

1'-0"

PLANK WITH GRIPS
ROUTED OUT

BENT METAL: TO
CLIP ONTO DOWELS

2x12 ADDED TO
2x12 TO GET THE
SAME EFFECT.

NOTES

WHEN USING PIPE, IT IS ADVISABLE TO PLUG UP THE ENDS OF THE PIPE TO PREVENT FINGERS GETTING STUCK. WHEN PIPES AND DOWELS ARE USED, MAKE CERTAIN THEY ARE WIDE ENOUGH NOT TO POKE OUT A CHILD'S EYE — A MINIMUM OF 1½" IN DIAMETER IS RECOMMENDED.

WHEN USING CABLE, COVER IT WITH GARDEN HOSE OR USE VINYL-COATED CABLE. NEVER USE A CABLE SO THIN THAT A CHILD CANNOT GRASP IT EASILY. A MINIMUM OF 1½" IS RECOMMENDED.

NEVER FASTEN (NAIL OR SCREW) INTO THE END GRAIN OF WOOD AS IT HAS NO STRUCTURAL CAPABILITY IN THAT DIRECTION.

2'-0" TO 4'-0"

2 x 8

SPRINGS

CONC. PAD

1'-0" 1'-0"

3 x 12

SPRING

MAX. LENGTH 8'

CONC.

10"-12" DIA. LOG

SCOOP OUT TOP
FOR SEATS

FLATEN OUT BOTTOM
TO RECEIVE SPRING

"U" BOLT

2 x 8

2 x 4

SADDLE CLAMP
IS AN ALTER-
NATE FOR A
"U" BOLT

SPRING
PADS

$\frac{5}{8}$" TH. STEEL PLATE

(GROUND)

$\frac{1}{2}$" DIA. ANCHOR BOLT
CONC. PAD 2'-0"
DEEP.

CANVAS

WOOD DOWEL

HOOK

ELASTIC ROPE

METAL GROMMET

HEM

LINE OF STITCHING

(CANVAS)

POST

WOOD DOWEL

PAINT ON GRAPHICS

A VARIETY OF SHAPES CAN BE MADE.

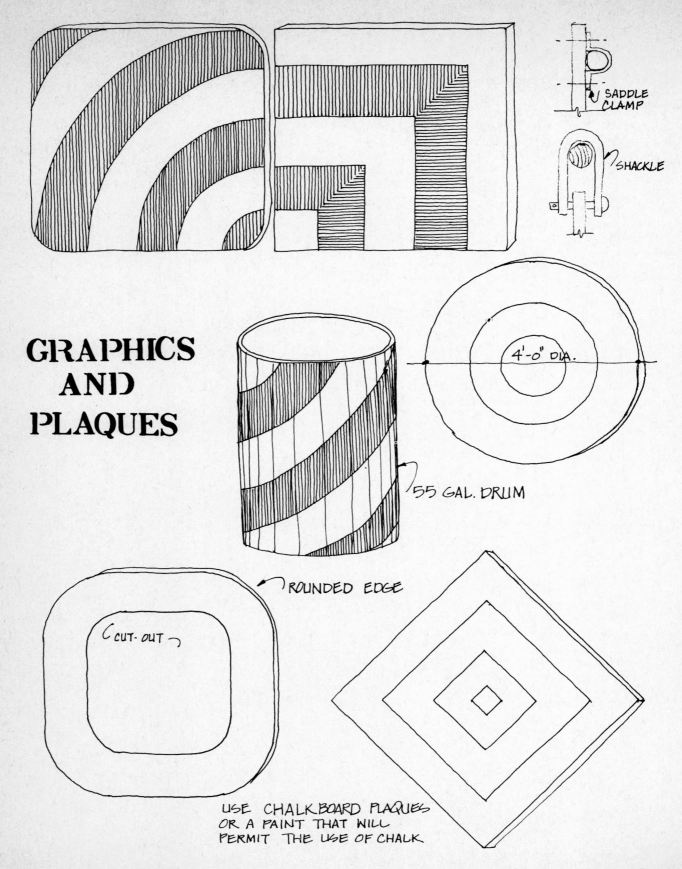

SADDLE CLAMP

SHACKLE

GRAPHICS AND PLAQUES

4'-0" DIA.

55 GAL. DRUM

ROUNDED EDGE

CUT-OUT

USE CHALKBOARD PLAQUES
OR A PAINT THAT WILL
PERMIT THE USE OF CHALK

GRAPHICS FOR ROLLING LOG & ROLLING BARREL

ROUNDED EDGE

CUT-OUT CIRCLE

CUT-OUT LADDER

CUT-OUT ARCH

24"

USE 3/4" OR 1" THICKNESS.

4' x 4' EXTERIOR GRADE PLYWOOD PAINT & CUT AS DESIRED.

THREADED PIPE CAP

FOUNTAIN PIPE

TAMPER-PROOF THREADED CAP.

DRILL SMALL HOLES IN PIPE

HOSE

1'x1'x1' CONC. FOOTING

BASE PIPE

HOSE CONNECTION

THREADED FLANGE W/ GASKET

HOSE

6x6, 8x8 OR 12x12 BURY 1'-0" BELOW GROUND

SPRINKLERS

WOOD OR PIPE POSTS

BENT PIPE

CONTINUOUS UNDERGROUND WATER SUPPLY PIPE

CONC. FOOTING

6' DIAM.

HEIGHT VARIES

HORIZONTAL RING OF SPRAY

102

FOUNTAINS

6×6, 8×8 10×10 OR 12×12

WATER SUPPLY PIPE

1½" × 1½" NOTCH W/ WOOD FILLER STRIP

BOLT TROUGHS TO COLUMNS

WOOD SCREW

6", 8", 10", 12"

2×6, 2×8 2×10 OR 2×12

BURY 3' BELOW GROUND

TROUGH DETAILS

½" CHAIN

8"-12" DIA. LOG

6x6, 8x8
OR 12x12

HOLE

BURY
2'-0"
BELOW
GROUND

ANIMALS

104

SCOOP OUT FOR SEAT

2×12

2×12

ROPE TAIL

LAG BOLT

12" DIA. LOG

8-10" DIA. LOG

BURY 2'

105

END
VIEW

½" DIA. BENT ROD

SADDLE CLAMP
OR PIPE CLAMP

106

PULL COVER OVER
SAND BOX & PEG
IN POSITION.

SAND BOXES BUILT
INTO WOOD DECKS.

SANDBOXES

2x6 DECK

2x8

2x4
NAILER

1x2

DECK

SAND

2x4

2x8

DETAIL

TO GET CORRECT
ANGLE, LAY OUT
PIECES & MARK
WITH A PENCIL

NOTCH EACH
PIECE HALF WAY

LAG BOLT PIECES
TOGETHER

FILL WITH SAND

108

● SAND, LIKE WATER, IS A RESPONSIVE ELEMENT WHICH ALLOWS A WIDE RANGE OF MANIPULATION AND SHOULD PERVADE THE PLAYGROUND RATHER THAN BEING CONTAINED IN A CONVENTIONAL BOX. SAND ALSO ACTS AS A BUFFER AND SHOULD BE PLACED AT THE BOTTOM OF SLIDES OR AT THE BASE OF SPRING PADS OR OTHER POINTS OF INTENSE ACTIVITY.

CHAMFER TOPS

12×12's VARY IN HEIGHT FROM 1'-0" TO 4'-0" ABOVE GROUND

SAND

12×12 TIMBERS LAG BOLTED TOGETHER

BURY 12×12's A FEW INCHES

THERE ARE NO LIMITS TO THE SIZE OR SHAPE OF THIS TYPE SAND BOX.

NOTES

WHEN USING ROPE OR CABLE, ALWAYS ANTICIPATE THAT A CERTAIN AMOUNT OF STRETCHING WILL OCCUR. PROVIDE FOR THIS BY CONSTANT TIGHTENING THROUGH THE USE OF TURNBUCKLES, EYE BOLTS, ETC.

MAKE SURE THAT ALL ELEMENTS IN THE PLAYGROUND THAT ARE SUPPOSED TO BE FIXED ARE RIGID. CHILDREN TEND TO EXPERIMENT WITH ANYTHING THAT MOVES AT ALL, AND CONSTANT JIGGLING OR SWINGING CAN BE DANGEROUS.

PLANTERS

3 × 8

2 × 10

2 × 10
4'-0" LONG

CLAY POT

2 × 2
NAILER

CUT A HALF CIRCLE
OUT OF EACH BOARD

NAIL ?

2 × 10's

LAG BOLT 4×4
PIECES TOGETHER

4×4's

2 × 10

2'-0" ±

LARGE
CLAY POT

PLAN

TOP 2×6

2×6   NAILER

3 - 4'

12-18"

TABLE

2×6

1" THICK MARINE
PLYWOOD

2×6   SCREW   GR.

4×4's

8"-24"

BOLT PIECES
TOGETHER

112

BENCHES

⅝" DIA. THREADED ROD

8" | 4" | 8"

6"

10"

12×12

BURY 2'-0"

COUNTERSINK WASHERS
& NUTS - PLUG WITH
WOOD DOWEL IF DESIRED

6×8

4×6

6"

12×12

THIS BENCH CAN BE
6' TO 12' LONG.

113

4', 6', 8'

2'

1'6"

4x6's

END LAP JOINT

½" DIA. THREADED
ROD W/ WASHER
& NUT ON EACH
END.

COUNTER SINK
HEXAGON NUT.
(WOOD PLUG
OPTIONAL)

SCREW INTO PIPE

3×8

"T" FITTING

1½" DIA. PIPE

2×4

SCREW

3×8

PIPE

2×4

2×12   SPAN   4'
3×12   "   6'
4×12   "   8'

WOOD SCREW

THREADED FLANGE

2½" PIPE BURIED 3' BELOW GROUND IN CONC. FOOTING

12" WIDE PLANK

LAG BOLT

LAG SCREW

2-STEEL ANGLES 4"×4"×¼"

3×4 LEGS

24" ±

1/4" SPACE

3 × 6's

BOLT

3×6

6" DIA. POST

16"

SECTION

BURY POST 18"

LAG BOLTS

6' LONG BENCH

21"

CHAMFER TOPS

4×4

2" DIA. HOLE FOR CHAIN & LOCK

LAG BOLT

2×4's

2½"

2'-0"

BIKE RACKS

3×6

3×6 SPACER

BOLT

3×6

3×6

3×6

NOTCH IN & TOE NAIL TOGETHER

7½" DIA. PIPE

3×6

2'-0"

3×6 SPACER

MATERIALS MATRIX

	Hardware Store	Lumber Yard	Chemical Co.	Garden Center	Service Station	Junk Yard	Marine Supply	Building Supply	Mail Order (Sears)	Plumbing Supply	Wire & Chain Co.	Telephone Co.	Awning Maker	Lighting/Utility Co.	Railroad	General Contractor	Auto Supply Co.	Sheet Metal Works	Demolished Bldg.
CHAIN	●						●				●								
FASTENERS: BOLTS, NAILS, SCREWS, ETC.	●	●					●	●	●										
55 GAL. DRUMS			●		●	●													
SPRINGS	●				●	●											●		
STAINLESS STEEL								●										●	
CANVAS							●						●						
PIPE	●						●			●									
HOSE	●			●						●									
ROPE	●						●												
CABLE & FASTENERS	●						●				●								
STEEL ANGLES/CHANNELS						●		●								●		●	
NETS	●						●	●											
CONCRETE BLOCK		●						●											●
LEACHING RINGS								●		●						●			
WOOD / LUMBER		●																	●
SPOOLS												●		●		●			
TELEPHONE POLES		●						●				●							
TIMBERS / R.R. TIES		●													●				●
FENCE	●			●				●											●
LADDERS	●	●						●											
DOWELS		●																	
WATER TANKS																			●
TIRES						●											●		
SCAFFOLDING								●								●			

HARDWARE

"S" HOOK

THREADED FLANGE

BRUSH

CHAIN

SHACKLE

SNAP SWIVAL HOOK

BENT ANGLE

HOOK

HINGE

MISSING LINK

FLAT ANGLE

SCREWS

ROUND HEAD

FLAT HEAD

NAILS

COMMON   FINISHING

TURNBUCKLE

HOOK   EYE

SCREW HOOK

SCREW EYE

LAG BOLT   CABLE CLAMP   'U' BOLT

CARRIAGE BOLT

SQ. NUT   HEX. NUT   CAP NUT

WASHER   LOCK WASHER

120

OPEN END WRENCH

HACK SAW

CARPENTERS SQUARE

HAMMER

RULE

SCREW-DRIVER

PLANE

LEVEL

COMBINATION SQUARE

PLIERS

CHISEL

TOOLS

BELT SANDER

BRACE & BIT

SAW

CIRCULAR SAW

PIPE WRENCH

DRILL

LEVEL

LOCKING PLIER WRENCH

IMPERIAL TO METRIC
CONVERSION TABLE

3/8"	=	9 MM
1/2"	=	12 MM
5/8"	=	15 MM
3/4"	=	18 MM
1"	=	25 MM
1 1/2"	=	38 MM
2"	=	50 MM
2 1/2"	=	65 MM
3"	=	75 MM
4"	=	100 MM
6"	=	150 MM
8"	=	200 MM
10"	=	250 MM
12"	=	300 MM
2'	=	600 MM
3'	=	900 MM
4'	=	1200 MM
5'	=	1500 MM
6'	=	1800 MM
8'	=	2500 MM
10'	=	3000 MM
12'	=	3600 MM
14'	=	4250 MM
16'	=	4800 MM

55 GALL DRUMS ARE
BRITISH 46 GALL (210 LITRE)

DO IT YOURSELF
PLAYGROUNDS